Let's Play Speech!

How to Give a Better Speech Using the Principles of Musical Performance

Emiko Hori

I can feel…

Music is my word

Word is my music

~~~ Emiko Hori

Contents

Prelude

Introduction

For many people, public speaking is scarier than death. When I started out as a speaker, I did not have this problem. Although I am not an extroverted person by nature, being in front of an audience was not a life or death situation for me. I began to wonder why. People kept telling me that I am good at presenting. People say I engage the audience. People say I own the stage. One day, I suddenly realized that my musical background as a concert pianist was a disguised foundation for being a good public speaker.

As a pianist, I've been educated at the Jacobs School of Music, Indiana University, one of the best music schools in the world. We were able to attend world-class concerts and operas every day for free. I learned numerous techniques of stage presence, delivery, and performance psychology at Indiana. I have toured throughout Europe as a part of the Schleswig-Holstein Music Festival Orchestra, Germany. I have performed in Canada and the US. I have mainly focused on touching people's hearts by performing at numerous castles, schools, private homes, and businesses.

In 2011, I gave a speech about the similarities between

music performance and public speaking. After receiving a wonderful response from the audience, I became motivated to help others, which led to this book.

Speech is a performance. I would like to share with you the musician's mindset, attitude and preparation for a performance. This mindset can apply to any presentation, any audience, and any circumstance.

This is a mini how-to book. It is a practical guide to applying musical principles to the delivery of a speech. I have strived to make this book be an easy read, where anybody can find the information they need (I use musical terms such as *movements* and *sections*) by flipping to any page of this book as a reference.

Obviously, this book alone cannot be the ultimate solution to being the world's greatest presenter. This is only the tip of the iceberg. However, these are core musical fundamentals that each one of us can quickly apply to prepare for a presentation in front of any audience. You don't even have to be a musician! If any of these *movements* enhance your next presentation, I will be delighted.

Lastly, I would like to say a special "thank you" to my teachers, Judy Carter, a humorist and the author of *The Comedy Bible* and *The Message Of You* and the 2001 World Champion of Public Speaking, Darren LaCroix. Judy's warm encouragement to integrate music into my presentation *and* Darren's openness to share his speaking world triggered me to go through this journey.

Let's Play Speech!

First Movement

On the Stage — A Musician's Approach

Did you know there are many similarities between piano performance and public speaking? They both have a clear message to deliver in front of the audience. They both impact the audience's life and way of thinking.

Interestingly, the musician's mindset seems to coincide with many aspects of public speaking. On the stage, what would musicians do? What would musicians think and feel? I am about to reveal this secret.

Section 1: The Stripper's Walk

You are about to be on center stage! You are energized, psyched. Your audience anticipates your grand appearance. Your host will announce your name and give an introduction. Then, all of a sudden, you are on the spot. You are walking onto the stage with enthusiasm.

But wait. Did you know that the first five seconds when you walk on the stage is the most critical part of your presentation? I call this "the Stripper's Walk." Stripper? What? You may argue that "I put on a nice suit for my presentation. I am not walking onstage naked!" It is the Stripper's Walk, because we are extremely vulnerable and completely exposed to the audience.

In these first five seconds, the audience will know exactly what you look like, your expressions, how tall or short you are, and most importantly, they will know *what kind of personality* you have, just by watching how you walk. Now that is scary.

For example, if in my first five seconds I present myself bent over, eyes wandering around with no focus, no smile, no sign of confidence, I will immediately lose credibility. People would see me as unprofessional. Unless my speech is about an old, insecure, and clumsy man, the audience will immediately reject me.

If I intend to perform piano music by Frederic Chopin, I cannot dash out onto the stage wearing my sneakers and say, "ta-da!" I have to set the tone for the music by walking rather gracefully, not running.

In most cases, we want to walk with confidence, head up, back straight, strong eye contact, big smile, and an engaging appearance. In order to keep my back straight, it always helps me to imagine somebody constantly pushing the middle point of my lower back slightly upward with his index finger.

Remember, we must *nail the audience* in the first five seconds!

Section 2: Listen — The Entire Body Becomes an Ear

There are multiple musical elements that I constantly use in my spoken presentations. For example, when I am presenting on the stage, my entire body becomes my ear. We all know that Mickey Mouse has two big ears. For me, that's not big enough!

Marek Jablonski, a famous Polish-Canadian pianist, told me one day, "We are responsible for what we create on the stage." And he was absolutely right!

On stage, when I play a phrase on the piano, I listen. For example, take the last phrase of the piano music, *Nocturne*, by Frederic Chopin. When I play it, I feel the sound carry to the back of the hall and bounce back to me. I listen. And I feel. Musicians are extremely sensitive to sound and acoustics. I feel the sound with every part of my body, not just with my ears.

I apply the same principle when I speak. While I am speaking, the audience usually listens quietly to my presentation. In that silence, I can listen and feel their unspoken response to my "music." Speech is not one-sided narration. Speech is communication.

I must be responsible for what I deliver by listening. I need to be sensitive to the audience reaction, also by listening.

For example, if the audience laughs at my remarks, I listen to their laughter bouncing off the walls and coming back to me. In that moment, my entire body becomes an ear, because I have to feel the precise moment to respond to the audience. If I don't listen and feel, I may interrupt their laughter. My presentation will not be as effective.

I picture a big smiley face in front of me while the audience is laughing. As the laughter gradually becomes softer and softer, my imaginary smiley face dissipates more and more. By associating a smiley face visually with the sound of laughter, it is easy for me to move forward. Once the imaginary smiley disappears, I resume speaking.

I listen to the audience's "wants" with my whole body, to achieve the best results in my presentation.

Section 3: Pause

Let's talk about the *pause*. In musical terminology, a pause is anticipation and a preparation for the next phrase.

In a musical sense, there is a phrase, and at the end of the phrase, there is a *cadence* (a definite harmonic resolution to conclude a section of music). Now I feel the resonance of the cadence. While feeling the resonance, I anticipate the next phrase.

Very interesting things happen when we musicians perform on stage. Let's take the example of a famous Russian composer and pianist, Sergei Rachmaninoff. He composed a series of *Piano Concerti*, piano music with orchestra. The beginning of his *Piano Concerto no. 2* starts with a series of massive chords. Depending upon the size of the hall, the time for the first chord to bounce back is different. The bigger the room, the longer it takes. After the first big chord, we cannot proceed to another chord while the first sound is still resonating. If two different kinds of sound happen simultaneously, it would be very confusing to the audience. It almost sounds like two bombs got thrown at you at the same time: boom, boom! Instead, the moment when the first chord dissipates becomes our pause.

The same thing happens with speech. If I say this to the audience, "Nancy, you look great!" (assuming Nancy is in the audience), I feel the word "great," and I especially feel the letter *t* at the end.

Then I anticipate the next phrase and imagine the first

word of the next sentence. After feeling the first word, I reposition myself in relation to audience and deliver the next phrase such as, "John, you look absolutely fabulous."

Following this principle, I felt the pause, the dissipation of the word "great." I felt the resonance of my cadence and the *t*-sound of the word "great."

You might be thinking: "But my voice does not resonate! How can I create dissipation in a speech?" Let's take the sentence "Nancy, you look great!" After feeling the *t* sound, we can picture this letter *t* in front of us. We can imagine that this letter slowly disappears from our sight. If we can visually sense the life of this letter and confirm *t* is no longer visible, we can move on. This precious moment becomes the pause.

If we cannot hear the sound resonating, a visual image gives us another spectrum to be aware of. With imagination, we can create customized pauses throughout our presentation.

Section 4: Measure

Do you know what a *measure* is in musical terms? A measure is the grouping of a specified number of musical beats located between two consecutive vertical lines on a staff. In other words, it is a metrical unit of music.

Marches by the famous American composer, John Philip Sousa (nicknamed "the March King"), have symmetrical measures, a total of four beats as one unit.

Sousa's marches are metrically constructed in four beats per measure: "1-2-3-4" "1-2-3-4." Sousa's music has a very steady beat so that people can easily walk with his music. Try walking with his music sometime!

Now imagine the concept of measure visually. Let's assume that there are four rectangular boxes (measures). Within each of the four boxes, there are four posts (see March – Symmetrical diagram). Let's march: "Left-Right-Left-Right" "1-2-3-4" "Left-Right-Left-Right" "1-2-3-4." Can you do that just by looking at this diagram? Great!

On the other hand, Frederic Chopin's music is asymmetrical. Let's take the same-sized four boxes. In Chopin's music, posts are not evenly distributed (see diagram). So, most of Chopin's music will sound like this: "1-2---3-4" "1----2-3-4" "1-2-3----4---."

Even though four posts exist in the same-sized four boxes, the asymmetrical arrangement makes a big difference in delivery.

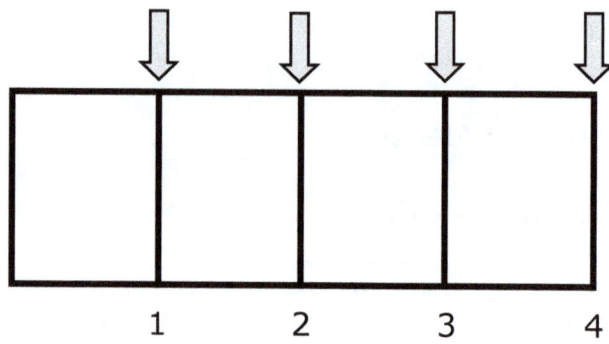

March - Symmetrical

You see, the distribution of posts and the distance between each post within a measure make a big difference in delivery. The same principle can be applied to a presentation. Taking the same sentence, we can create a big difference by either delivering it symmetrically or asymmetrically.

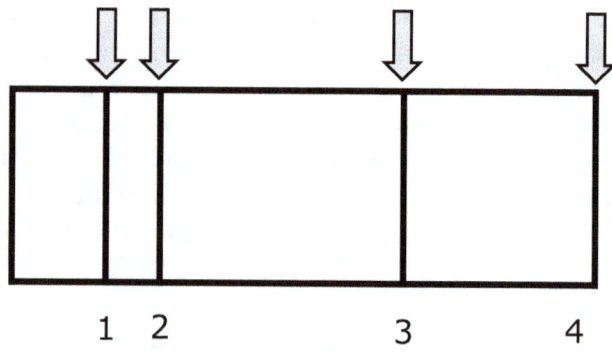

Chopin Waltz - Asymmetrical

Here is an example. There is a movie called *Crocodile Dundee*. In this movie, when Crocodile Dundee is confronted with a New York mugger armed with a knife, he pulls out his own two-foot knife and says, "Now that's a knife." He does not say "Left-Right-Left-Right" "Now-that's-a-knife." Rather he says, "Now that's — a knife."

Can you say the same phrase above in a symmetrical way? If you can deliver in two different ways, congratulations. If you can deliver in multiple ways, that is even better. Depending upon the emphasis you want to make, measure makes a huge impact in the delivery of your presentation.

Section 5: Posture

Some people believe that a pianist plays the piano with just ten fingers. Actually, in order to play the piano, we must use the entire body. Both feet stay solid, pushing firmly on the floor. Our back should be straight, but the spine needs to be flexible.

The arm is an extension of the back. The arms need to be relaxed, with shoulders and elbows loose and wide. The neck is also relaxed, not bent in an awkward position.

The hand is an extension of the arm. The hands and fingers should be supple but firm. When the pianist plays a big chord of, say Rachmaninoff, it requires a concentrated effort to use all of the body parts, not just pushing ten fingers onto the keyboard, but throwing the back and arms into the act as well.

When we are performing piano on stage, the focal point is on our lower back, as if large, solid, invisible hands are supporting the lower back and waist, pushing us straight forward.

There was a time that I used to practice piano five to six hours a day every day to prepare for concerts. I practiced even longer on the day before the concert. When I was not making a conscious effort to use my entire body and practicing with a "bad" posture—say no lower back support and no relaxed shoulders and arms— my fingers got tired very easily. My ten fingers were straining and carrying an extra weight which should have been carried by my lower back.

This can also be caused by an improperly positioned piano bench. If the piano bench is positioned too low, my arms are positioned upward from the elbow to the keyboard. This position is not desirable when I need to play a big chord. By shifting my weight onto my elbow, I was forcing my fingers to push the keys with unnecessarily effort. This could result in hurting my fingers, my neck, and my arm.

By the same token, in order to speak profoundly, we must use our entire body to express our words. Singers use their diaphragm to breathe, inhale, and exhale. Just like singers, speakers need to stand tall, shoulders wide. Good positioning of feet, legs, and arms is a must. Speakers also need to have good back support to generate a strong voice. If we try to project our voice from just the throat, the sound will not carry through to the back of the room. We must speak with our entire body.

You might say that since we can use a microphone, we don't have to worry about these factors. However, even when using a microphone, if our posture is not aligned correctly, we cannot generate the strong, confident voice that the audience likes to hear. Even when we walk on to and off the stage, it is best to make the effort to walk supported by the lower back.

Posture. Are you fully aware of yours on the stage?

Section 6: Feeling

How can we make our music performance engaging and interesting? We must have feelings, not just simply memorize notes and rhythm.

For example, Robert Schumann, a great German pianist and composer, composed a piece in 1839 called *Fantasie in C*. This music has its origin in early 1836, when Schumann composed a piece entitled *Ruines*, expressing his distress at being parted from his beloved Clara Wieck (who later became his wife).

In order to achieve the feeling of *Fantasie in C*, musicians perform with despair, sadness, and longing for reunion with the loved one. When I performed this music, I had to apply my own despair and longing for reunion with the loved one—my grandfather. He passed away in 1995 after stroke. After a long, thirteen-hour-flight to Japan from San Francisco, I was tired and exhausted. Then, immediately, I had to face the death of a person I admired in my life. No matter how much I longed for him, he will never come back to us again.

On the stage, I cannot simply mechanically push eighty-eight piano keys and hope to resonate with the audience. I have to recreate feelings I have experienced in the past, such as despair, sadness, and loneliness. In order to express sadness on the piano, usually I listen to sad-sounding chords (usually in a *minor* key), approach the piece slowly, and gently play these chords as if my fingers are crying. If I do not express these feelings through the music, it will probably sound boring, rather than compelling. On the contrary, I cannot play a sad-sounding chord with a happy face, either. I guarantee that people would walk out the door within the first five minutes.

In the same way, in our speeches, we need to express our feelings to make our presentation engaging and interesting. For instance, there are thousands of ways to say this phrase on the stage: "Mother, I love you."

What is your emotion when you say the phrase above?

1. Happiness?
2. Sadness?
3. Anxiety?
4. Boredom?
5. Depression?
6. Fear?
7. Hope?
8. Joy?
9. Passion?
10. Excitement?

Can you say the phrase "Mother, I love you" ten different ways or more? Where do these emotions come from?

If you can express your feelings in a variety of ways, congratulations. These emotions do not come from acting. These emotions come from our own heart. Furthermore, genuine feelings need to come from that moment in our past when we actually said to our own mother, "Mother, I love you."

If we intend to express "happiness" and the audience does not feel the same, our delivery is not successful.

How do you express your feelings on the stage? How do you feel happiness on the stage? Be in that moment by feeling as you did in your past. If you are in that moment, the audience will share the moment with you.

Section 7: Tonality

As a cellist would say, the sound of the musical note C fluctuates, depending upon the *tonality* of the entire music. If the entire piece of music is in a *major key* (a happy musical tone), cellists will adjust the tonality of C with a bright, cheerful pitch, measured in Hertz, or cycles per second. If it is in a minor key (a sad musical tone), cellists will tune the instrument and adjust the C sound by a hair to a flat, lower pitch. If it is a subtle, small-enough adjustment, the audience will not notice that it is flat.

I wish I could do similar adjustments with a piano on the stage! This is nearly impossible unless:

1. I bring my piano tuner on the stage, make him sit next to me during my performance, and say: "Mr. Tuner, here it is! Quick! Tighten this note while I am playing an octave lower!"

2. I hold a series of wrenches during the performance on the stage, which is not possible!

I do not mean to be too technical here. In fact, tonality is closely related to feeling. In Section 6, we talked about feeling. Feeling comes as a reaction to a certain event. Inner forces within us will trigger feeling(s) in response to a certain incident. This inner force will generate our voice, influencing our presentation.

Now, tonality can be improved by taking it to the next

level of competency. How would you diagnose and analyze your inner force and perfect your delivery?

Let's go back to the last phrase: "Mother, I love you." Let's assume that we want excitement within this phrase. We imagine the day when we actually said this to our mother with excitement. Now say it with excitement. Good. But wait, what type of excitement? The tonality of a voice may differ in different situations:

- I said this when I was five years old when my mother baked my favorite cookie.
- I said this when I was a teenager and reconciled with her after a disagreement.
- I said this when I was accepted at the university of my choice.
- I said this when she was in the hospital, and I was trying to cheer her up.
- I said this while holding a bouquet of flowers on her fiftieth birthday.

What is your tonality when you say, "Mother, I love you?" If I am speaking as a five-year-old, I might raise my tone slightly higher. If my mother is in the hospital, I would show concern with a slightly lower pitch. Are you fully aware of your tonality? Tonality must fluctuate depending on the different types of feelings you are delivering on the stage.

Section 8: Breathing

In music, each phrase has a life cycle: beginning, climax, and ending. In order to begin a phrase, we need to prepare by taking a breath. The way we prepare to breathe corresponds with the *tempo* (speed) of the phrase. If the phrase is quick and whimsical, then we take a quick breath before we perform the phrase. On the other hand, if the phrase is slow, long, and relaxed, then we take a long, relaxed breath before we perform.

Breathing is not just for singers. All musicians breathe in order to perform. Pianists take a big breath prior to perform a massive chord of Rachmaninoff. They take a long, gentle breath prior to performing a soft, delicate *Nocturne* of Chopin. Pianists also breathe together with other musicians when they play in ensembles. Not only do we breathe together, we make sure that in each phrase's life cycle, we begin our phrases together and end them together.

When I was performing a trio (three musicians in an ensemble), I met with the other two musicians, a cellist and a violinist, and we trained ourselves to count together silently from one to twenty. We counted one number per second, without saying a word. If we matched our breathing, as we counted silently, after counting to twenty, we began the music together. If we did not match our breathing, after counting to twenty, we did not begin together, and the ensemble was not successful. I have to admit, this exercise was not an easy task for any of us.

When we first started this exercise, all of us were counting based on our own assumptions and could not match our breathing at all. As time progressed, we noticed a difference. Before we inhaled, we looked at each other and gave a signal to start. We made a conscious effort to breathe together by observing each other's eyes and body language. By repeating this exercise, not only could we count and breathe together, but we also started to feel the music together by being aware of each other's breathing.

How do you breathe before you speak a word? We usually don't count numbers, and we don't analyze how we breathe. However, even if only by second nature, a slight conscious effort will make a big difference in our presentation.

If we intend to present a serious subject, such as a tragedy in life, we cannot take a quick breath before presenting. The deeper the personal story, the more desirable it is to breathe more slowly and deeply in order to set the tone.

On the other hand, when we share our excitement and happiness, enthusiasm cannot be sustained with slow breathing. Yes! We can be enthusiastic when speaking and take a quick breath as necessary.

Have you ever visualized your own breathing? I usually conduct my breathing with my arms, just like conductors conducting a symphony. When I inhale, I raise my arms. After I complete the inhale, I stop and keep my arms up high. When I exhale, I slowly lower my arms. I am not saying you need to physically move your arms up and down in front of the audience. But try practicing this before your presentation.

The slower your arm movements, the more intimate

the conversation becomes. The faster your arm movements, the more energized you become. Once you are accustomed to this visualization, you can do the same breathing exercise without raising your arms. If you can "visualize" your arm movement without actually raising your arm, you are in control of your breathing.

Visualization of breathing can be applied at various speeds. That is what conductors do. As I mentioned before, the most important aspect of breathing is how we prepare. For slow breathing, we prepare to breathe slowly. For a fast and exciting part of the presentation, we prepare to breathe quickly.

Breathing is a critical part of presenting. Experiment with it to find the best ways to breathe in your presentation.

Section 9: Touch

What is your *touch*? Do you make your audience happy with certain delivery styles? Do you mesmerize your audience with a mellow voice?

Playing piano is not just pushing eighty-eight black and white keys. When I play the music of Claude Debussy, the French impressionist composer in the early 1900s, my fingers will touch the key horizontally as if they are light feathers. I am talking about Debussy's music *Images pour Piano, Reflets dans l'eau* (Reflections on the water). As my fingers lightly glide over the keyboard, as if they were feathers moving across the surface of the water, the sound becomes soft, velvety, and colorful.

When pianists perform piano music of the famous German composer, Beethoven, as you can probably guess, our fingers cannot be as light as feathers. For the music of Beethoven, pianists play with authority, with preciseness of rhythm in grand chords. Each of the fingers will walk on the keyboard like a macho man.

I mentioned feeling and tonality earlier. Let's consider the phrase one more time: "Mother, I love you."

What is your touch for this presentation? I don't mean you need to literally "touch" somebody in the audience. Different touch creates a different texture. Here are some possibilities:

- "Mother, I love you" (being said by a five-year-old, with enthusiasm)

- Open arms, roll the eyes, raise eye contact level higher as if a five-year-old talking to mother
- Bring cookies as a prop (if possible)
- Say "Mother" enthusiastically, open arms, roll the eyes, then tone down with your mellow voice saying "I love you"

Other possibilities:

- Bring your mother into the audience and deliver to her in real time
- Present a video of your mother
- Present a picture of your mother
- Present a voice recorder (such as an MP3) of your mother
- Talk to a fictitious mother, looking higher than the eye level of the audience
- Talk to a fictitious mother, someone in the audience, as if she is your mother
- Talk to a fictitious mother on the stage next to you
- Bring a bouquet of flowers as a prop and say it

The possibilities are endless. What is your "touch?"

Section 10: Take-Away

What is the take-away message in your presentation? In music, musicians build up to a certain take-away theme, and bang! When the music comes to the climax, musicians sustain the energy of the excitement, depending upon how long this occurs. Sustaining the energy of the take-away requires both mental and physical strength.

In our presentation, it is boring to give the take-away message at the very beginning. It is more desirable to save it to the middle or toward the end. If you give away everything in the first sentence, people can walk out of the door.

If we use the same take-away phrases repeatedly throughout our presentation, we should present them differently the second time. We don't want to deliver the same phrase the same way, over and over. In music, when I play repeated phrases on the piano, I make a conscious effort to differentiate them.

For the next round of the same phrase, I:

- Slow down the beginning
- Slow down the ending
- Start stronger in the beginning
- End stronger in the ending
- Take longer pauses between each phrase
- Take shorter pauses between each phrase
- Emphasize louder and slower an entire phrase

- Emphasize softer and slower an entire phrase
- Emphasize softer and faster an entire phrase
- Emphasize louder and faster an entire phrase
- Play an octave (eight pitches) higher than original, if allowed
- Play an octave lower than original, if allowed

There can be more! There are unlimited possibilities and options. What is your take-away and where? How would you approach it?

Let's Play Speech!

Second Movement

How to Prepare Part 1 — A Musician's Mindset

Pianists are experts at preparation, or practice. One of the reasons why pianists are rigorous about preparation is that we are forced to memorize our music on stage.

During the course of practice and live performance, I have spent countless hours memorizing pieces of music. Sometimes I found myself practicing five to six hours a day, staring at the same passages over and over. Was this memorization routine beneficial? I often wished I was perfect and did not need to practice anything. I often wrongly told myself that my precious time had been "wasted."

Now as I look back, I am convinced that the time I spent on memorization was not wasted. I can apply this process of preparation to any presentation, using the pianist's mindset. Even though I don't memorize every single presentation, I take preparation very seriously. I hope you do too.

Section 1: The 120/80 Principle

How do you prepare for your presentation? In the music world, we have the 120/80 principle. That means if I prepare 120 percent of what I want to accomplish on the stage, the outcome will be about 80 percent of what was expected.

The reason why we say 120/80 is that during the live presentation, a number of things may happen on stage:

- Issues with the microphone
- Forgetting a line
- Unexpected audience response
- Unexpected distraction
- Condition of the stage (e.g., the floor makes noise when someone walks on it)
- Forgetting props
- …and so on

Just ask any presenter or performer after the presentation if they achieved 100 percent of the goal of their performance. Nearly all would say no. There is always room for improvement!

In terms of piano practice and performance, there is no such thing as "over-rehearsing." There is always something to improve on. Within a short, single phrase in music, there are thousands of ways to interpret and express it. Just imagine the millions of combinations and possibilities that can be demonstrated in a ten-minute presentation. It is impossible to over-rehearse millions of options.

Another factor is that when you start practicing your presentation, there might be an interruption. The phone may start ringing, a guest may suddenly come over, kids are bugging you, friends are nagging you, parents are screaming, and so on. How can you sustain your practice session in spite of these obstacles?

Sometimes you have to put yourself in a physical location where no interruption will happen for the time allocated for your presentation. Lock yourself in your room, escape to a friend's place, the backyard, a garage, gym, basement, school, office, or even the bathroom! You must be creative in finding where you want to rehearse. Then run through your presentation from beginning to end, without stopping.

One day, I snuck into a conference room where I was to give a speech the following day. Even though I was allowed to rehearse on the day of the presentation, I wanted to see if I could get an additional practice in prior to my allocated time. It was a large amphitheater-style auditorium in a hospital. Luckily, the door was unlocked, and the facility manager graciously let me in. I gave my entire presentation for the facility manager, without stopping from beginning to end. I was extremely fortunate to have this opportunity.

However, most of the time, we are not that lucky. We have no guarantee of securing a conference room whenever we want to rehearse. Then, we have to be creative.

Be sure to situate yourself in the center of the room where you are practicing. Next, feel the size of the actual stage you will be presenting on. You have to imagine that the room you practice in is the size of the stage where you'll be giving the presentation. This is necessary for a successful practice session. It requires tremendous concentration, effort, and imagination. It must all be in your head—what the space looks like, how big the space is, and so on. But it works. Can you imagine yourself standing alone in the middle of Rose Bowl Stadium giving a presentation to ninety thousand people? Good. If you can imagine this, you are on the right track.

Give your presentation from beginning to end, without stopping. How do you feel after going over your presentation? Being able to rehearse the presentation without stopping is the minimum requirement prior to giving a real presentation. Did you feel that you nailed it 100 percent? If so, congratulations. You must feel good about it. You should be proud of yourself for achieving it. However, at the same time, you may need more work until you feel your presentation is 120 percent ready.

You may want to analyze which section needs to be refined. Once you figure it out, you may want to practice your presentation separately in smaller modules. Sometimes you may want to practice just the conclusion multiple times. Sometimes you may want to practice just the middle section several times.

Have you noticed that a great musicians' CD sounds so perfect no matter where you start listening, even from the middle of the phrase? This is not because of the effect of professional editing. Rather, it is because of the result of delivering the music with 120 percent conviction.

You may want to record or videotape your practice session, from beginning to end. Then listen to your recording from the middle of your speech, from the middle of your sentence. Did your delivery sound natural to you? If not, something may not be quite refined enough.

Remember, the 120/80 principle is the key to successful preparation.

Section 2: Imagination

What can you picture in your mind while you give your presentation? Let's go back to Debussy's *Images pour Piano, Reflets dans l'eau.* While I play this music, I imagine a serene nature scene—a quiet pond surrounded by large, lush, and mature trees. It is early morning in spring time. Sunshine is just about to peek over the horizon. Several maple trees are casting shadows over the pond. There are about twenty large water lilies floating gently and peacefully on the surface. Then dew drops suddenly fall from a maple tree branch onto the pond, creating small circles and changing the shapes in the water. The water lilies are dancing slowly, in time with the waves. The water is sparkling in the sunlight. Nobody else is there. There is nothing but peace...

Why does imagination succeed in creating music? Imagination draws pictures and visual images in our mind. If, instead of the previous scene in preparation for playing *Images pour piano, Reflets dans l'eau*, I imagine a stormy night, my performance will sound much more aggressive, and I will feel more agitated (which is not an accurate interpretation of this particular piece of music).

To take another example, consider Rachmaninoff. In order to perform his piano music successfully, we may choose to (but not be limited by) imagining a rich, dense, chocolate cake. With Rachmaninoff's rich, massive, heavy chords and tonality, his music cannot be imagined as delicate, fluffy, white angel food cake. I hope you can feel and taste the differences between dense chocolate cake and fluffy angel cake. How do you feel music as a rich chocolate cake? Every person may feel this differently; however, it certainly won't feel like (or taste like) whipped cream over a light sponge cake.

You can practice your presentation without saying a word. Imagination can be a vehicle for us as presenters to be in a particular mindset, at that particular moment of the speech. Imagination can also control our emotion.

You can practice internally, closing your eyes. Imagine how you stand on the stage. How would you visualize certain parts of your presentation? Can you see the visual images with your eyes closed? If yes, you are on the right track. If no, you may want to practice with your eyes closed until you start seeing the images.

Here are other elements that you may want to consider as you continue your imagination exercises.

Can you imagine the faces of the characters in your presentation?

- Happy?
- Sad?
- Energized?
- Angry?
- Confused?

Can you feel the air move?

- Cold air, coming from where?
- Warm air, coming from where?
- Is the window open in the scene?
- Is the door open?

- How warm or cold is it?

Do you feel the sunshine in the room?

- Where is the sunshine coming from?
- Where on your body do you feel the sunshine?
- How bright is the sunshine?
- Is it raining or snowing instead?

Can you picture the location of your characters?

- Is it indoors?
- Is it outdoors?
- Which city or country?
- What time of the day is it?

Do you see your characters in your presentation in further detail?

- Do you see the facial expressions of your characters?
- Do you see the activities of your characters?
- Do you feel the emotions of your characters?
- How far or close are you from your characters?

Can you imagine all this while closing your eyes? When you use imagination effectively as a part of your preparation, you will certainly see and feel the difference when you are live on stage. The more you can imagine your presentation internally and the more you can mentally prepare for it, the more your audience will experience the same sensations with you and the more effectively you can take them on your journey.

Section 3: Mirror, Mirror

Mirror, mirror on the wall…no, I am not Snow White. Rather, I practice my presentation with a mirror. As you may already know, this is a controversial topic. The mirror: some love it, some hate it. I have to admit, I would go completely insane if I had to look at myself in the mirror during my presentation. It would be very distracting. I am vulnerable in front of a mirror, thinking:

"Oh, I am so ugly!"

"Gee, I am incredibly short."

"My goodness, I look clumsy."

I'm the worst judge of my own body. I could not concentrate on my presentation.

However, the mirror is a healthy tool in a practice session, if used sporadically and effectively. I usually place my tall, wooden-framed mirror, resting on the wall next to my piano. I position it to my side where I can see my piano stool and my body.

Before I practice the piano, I check my posture: the position of my back, feet, arms, and shoulders. I also check my hand positions before and after I take a big leap from note to note. Why? Because if the lower half of my body is not aligned properly, most of the time my fingers and arms are not in the desired position. In that case, I may either hit the wrong notes or create an unwanted sound effect. By checking the mirror occasionally, I can correct bad habits. Yes, the mirror is not just for dancers anymore.

I remember when I was practicing Debussy's *Reflets dans leau*, there was one passage in the music that I struggled with; I could not express the reflection on the water! I spent hours pounding on the keyboard and could not figure out what was wrong. It sounded very heavy and dead, almost like mud, not water. Then, I glanced at myself at the mirror and realized that my right arm and the position of my elbow were too low to maneuver. After correcting the position of my arm, I gained freedom in my wrist and fingers.

For my speech practice, I usually place the tall mirror in the center of the room. I check my posture at the beginning and at the ending of my presentation. I do not practice an entire presentation using the mirror. I use it to check positioning, and spend no more than five to ten seconds glancing at it.

A mirror is especially helpful when we use props. We can check the following:

- How the prop will look on us or with us?
- How do we introduce the prop on the stage?
- How big or small is the prop?
- When do we use the prop?
- When do we not use the prop?
- How flawlessly do we handle the prop?
- How can we incorporate the prop with the right words, sentences, and pauses?
- How do we pick up the prop while we are speaking?
- From which area of the stage do we pick up the prop while speaking?

- How do we place the prop on the stage while speaking?
- …and so on.

A mirror is also helpful when we need to check the following:

- Within the first five seconds of the "Stripper's Walk" (from the First Movement), how am I walking?
- Posture
- Facial expressions (e.g., happiness, sadness, anger)
- Change in the facial expression from section to section of the presentation while speaking
- Pauses
- Hand gestures incorporated with facial expressions
- Eye contact
- Dialogue, especially positioning of characters
- Movement during transition
- Final check of the clothes we plan to wear on stage

The list can continue endlessly. When we use the mirror effectively, it will become our best friend and a powerful coach.

Mirror, mirror, you are incredible!

Section 4: Rhythm

Musicians feel rhythm all day, throughout the day. In music terminology, there are several categories which differentiate types of rhythm:

- March: a piece of music, usually in four beats to the bar, having a strongly accented rhythm for walking.
- Polka: a lively couple-dance of Bohemian origin, with music in two meter.
- Waltz: a piece of music for, or in the rhythm of a ballroom dance, in moderately fast triple meter, in which the dancers revolve in perpetual circles, taking one step to each beat.
- Rap: a style of popular music, developed by disc jockeys and urban blacks in the late 1970s, in which an insistent, recurring beat pattern provides the background and counterpoint for rapid, slangy, and often boastful rhyming patter glibly intoned by a vocalist or vocalists.
- Tango: a ballroom dance of Latin-American origin, danced by couples, and having many varied steps, figures, and poses.
- Jazz: music originating in New Orleans around the beginning of the twentieth century and subsequently developed through various increasingly complex styles, generally marked by

intricate rhythms, polyphonic (many sounds at once) ensemble playing, and improvisatory patterns.

- …and so on.

Musicians make an effort to vary a repetitive rhythmic pattern. If we plan to present the exact same musical rhythm three times, for example, Chopin's Waltz, we strive to present it in three different ways. Do you remember symmetrical and asymmetrical measures in the First Movement, Section 4? It is a similar concept here for rhythm. Unless we vary the rhythm, an audience will know immediately that the same pattern is coming back again and again.

You don't have to be a musician to feel rhythm. Rhythms are everywhere in our daily life, such as:

- Clock ticking
- Washer and dryer spinning
- Traffic lights (synchronized light movements)
- Car horn
- Phone ring-tone
- Cheerleaders dancing
- Rain dropping from the roof
- Car engine idling
- Dew dripping from the tree
- Cat's collar bell ringing
- Olympic athletes (swimming strokes, floor work, figure skating, alpine skiing movements, etc.)

We listen to rhythm. We walk with rhythm. We speak

with rhythm. What is the rhythm of your daily life?

As you may already know, a repetitive rhythm for a long period of time will eventually put an audience to sleep. For example, let's take a look at the phrase below. Can you say this phrase in the same *pitch* (tone of sound), same rhythm, and same speed from one to five hundred?

"One Sheep
Two Sheep
Three Sheep
Four Sheep
Five Sheep"

How was it? You can easily guess the outcome. On the stage, repetitive phrases will put the audience to sleep unless you vary the pattern of rhythm, pitch, or speed. Let's go back to these sheep above and present this with five completely different rhythms (and even with different **facial expressions**) such as:

"O-ne Sheeeeep (**happy**),
Twoooo Shhhhheep (**sad**),
Three [long pause] Sheep (**fearful**),
F-o-u-r S-h-e-e-p (**angry**),
Five Sheep (**sleepy**)"

This will pique the audience's curiosity.

As a performer, we want to create unpredictability in our presentation. When we can create more unpredictability, it is more satisfying to the audience.

How can we apply this rhythm variance to our speech? These are some possibilities:

- Avoid a repetitive rhythm (or phrase) if possible
- On two identical rhythms, add emphasis and slow down the second time
- On two identical rhythms, take longer pauses before saying it the second time
- Rhyme the main rhythm differently the second time (i.e., "Cat is on the mat" vs. "Dog is on the Bobcat")

Another way to vary rhythm is to follow your own footsteps. Unless we are robots, the distance of each step between one foot and the another is not exactly the same. Let's experiment with this sentence: "Hi! How are you?"

Can you say this while you are walking normally? There are several ways to say this:

- Say each word per step
- Say each word per two steps
- Say the first word per step ("Hi"), then each additional word per two steps
- Say each word per four steps

Did you feel the difference in rhythm? There are thousands of combinations by varying how fast or slow you walk each step, how high or low you say each word. A word of caution: I am not trying to teach acting or singing. These are just suggestions about how to practice various rhythms in a sentence. By breaking a normal speaking habit, you may be able to discover new rhythmic patterns that you want to adopt in your speech.

Section 5: How to Get There

On a piano keyboard, there is a long range from the lowest *A* key to the highest *C*. This is the distance of the keyboard, a total of eighty-eight keys on the piano. It is extremely rare to play from the lowest *A* sound to the highest C within a single piece of music. However, on some occasions, we pianists have to play the distance from point A to point B in one big leap. When that happens, we have to imagine as if the arm is creating an arc from point A to point B.

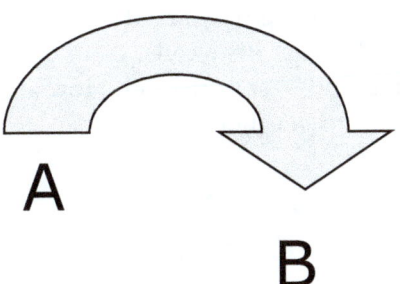

A
B

An Imaginary Arc

Why an arc? Because it is the most natural movement of the human body. Please imagine a conductor on the podium. He or she usually follows a gentle curve with his or her hands and arms to express the music. If this line is straight, the hand movement will be rigid and very mechanical. The music may also sound rigid and mechanical.

An imaginary arc. For my speech, I picture this arc in my mind whenever I need to:

- Walk up to shake somebody's hand on stage
- Change the scene or location in my speech from point A to point B
- Move to the next module in my speech

By picturing it, I can draw an imaginary three-dimensional line on stage. In that way, I follow the line and I am able to physically aim at my final destination. I see a gentle circular imaginary arc. This image works very well in my presentation. Physically, I can create a smooth transition, not a rigid, fast transition. How about you? How do *you* want to get there?

Section 6: How to Practice

When we are deep into the performance and our interpretation of the music, our mind does not have time for distraction.

Longer practices do not always mean better practices. In fact, meaningless practice for a long period of time is counterintuitive and harmful. Practicing without total concentration is a meaningless activity.

However, given human nature, distraction is unavoidable in our daily life.

- "Here comes my Mom. I have to check what she has to say."
- "Oh, my cell phone is ringing. It must be urgent."
- "I have no time! My friend is looking for me right now!"

We have to deal with daily activities, parents, friends, siblings, significant others—you name it.

As I mentioned earlier in Section 1, the 120/80 principle is all about dedicating 120 percent of effort to create an 80 percent result. In order to achieve this level of dedication, here is a trick. Allocate five minutes of your time to be alone. Hide somewhere from friends and family. Lock yourself in for five minutes without any distractions. That will give you enough time to deeply explore your presentation for five minutes. Effective time management is the key to success.

Five minutes of total concentration is an enormous effort. I am not sure if you are aware of it, but a human concentration span can be as short as eight seconds. Only eight seconds!

I get extremely tired mentally after five minutes of 100 percent concentrated work on the piano. You may think it is just piano playing. No, that is not true.

Hide yourself away for five minutes somewhere. Fully devote your energy to your presentation for five minutes. How can you do that? Here is the checklist:

- Make sure you are alone for five minutes
- Have your presentation material ready
- Decide which segment of a module you want to "drill" for three to four minutes
- Without stopping and without thinking about anything else, imagine yourself on stage
- Picture yourself giving a presentation
- Take a deep breath (for relaxation)
- Go over your three- to four-minute segment in real-time without stopping
- Find out in which section you became distracted in during this three- to four-minute segment
- Find out what you were thinking when you were distracted (e.g., suddenly started thinking about tonight's dinner, work, a friend, a chore for the day, etc.)
- Brainstorm "why" you started thinking about unrelated activities
- Find the best solution(s) not to be distracted for the next time you practice this three- to four-minute segment

- Does the interruption always occur at the same phrase or sentence of the module?
  - If "Yes," then your presentation material may need some work and improvement
  - If "No," then focus on concentrating so as not to think about anything else

If you are not focusing, don't practice until the next opportunity comes. Otherwise, it is not an effective practice. There is a Japanese story about a monk's pupil who has been told not to think about rabbits. During the meditation, guess what the pupil was thinking about? That's right. The rabbits.

Five minutes' concentration in which you are not thinking about a certain object requires discipline and practice. All musicians learn this discipline through education and training. However, you don't need to be a musician to do this. It is a matter of practicing this mental exercise as often as possible. If you take the initiative to do it, you'll be surprised at how much more effectively you'll be able to focus on the stage.

Section 7: Planning for the Unexpected—"What If…"

Creating a mental list of unexpected incidents that might occur on stage is part of the preparation. In the back of my mind, I always have this: "What if…"

It is a mindset, an adaptation of a quick response in case of emergency. Mishaps sometimes happen in a musical performance. There is a famous story about Midori, a world-renowned Japanese violinist. In 1986, she gave her legendary performance at Tanglewood, during which she broke one of the strings of her own violin (the E-string, to be exact). During the performance, she borrowed the Concertmaster's violin and continued performing. About thirty seconds later, she broke the E-string once again. She finished her performance with the Associate Concertmaster's violin. The next day, the *New York Times* carried the headline: "Girl, 14, Conquers Tanglewood with 3 violins."

Speaking of mishaps, what do you suppose I do if I forget a note during my piano performance? I just move on. The performance need to be flawless, just like riding on a moving escalator from the first floor to the second floor without stopping. There is no going back. As long as I am musically correct in terms of interpretation, I will succeed in engaging the audience despite a few missed notes. Usually, the audience is forgiving about a small mistake or two, or may not even notice you missed the notes. By the end of the performance, they will usually forget them. On the other hand, if I am not musically correct and I'm not engaging the audience, they will spot my flaws right away.

How can we apply this principle to a speech? Listing the possibilities for unexpected mishaps ahead of time helps when incidents actually happen. Here are some of the examples:

What if…

- I forget the first line of my speech?
- The audience doesn't laugh at my punch line?
- I forget to bring my prop?
- I accidentally drop my prop during the presentation?
- I cannot take my hat off my head during the speech (assuming that my hat is my prop)?
- I cannot find a table to place my hat (or any of my props)?
- My PowerPoint does not start?
- My laptop is dead?
- The room is too hot?
- My microphone does not function?
- The room has no microphone?
- An audience member's cell phone rings?
- The stage makes noise when I walk around?
- …and so on

During the preparation, it is ideal to make a mental note (or write them down if you want to be totally sure) of what to do in every one of the scenarios above.

If an accident happens on the stage, then...

- I improvise on Module A with plan B or ask my audience "Where was I?"
- I kick my hat and say "C"
- I leave my hat on my head and move on to Module B
- I place my hat on the floor and say "X"
- I make sure have a copy of my PowerPoint on a flash drive
- I make sure that I wear layers of clothes to adjust the temperature
- I bring my own microphone or I am prepared to speak loudly
- I have prepared a joke about cell phones that acknowledges the distraction and moves on
- Make sure to inspect the stage beforehand to avoid mistakenly walking on a weak spot of the stage
- ...and so on

These are called "planned" spontaneous actions. It is like a fire drill. Keep a mental note in the back of your mind, and use it if necessary. We all hope that nothing unexpected happens on stage. If something *does* happen, well, you are 120 percent ready to take alternate action!

Third Movement

How to Prepare Part 2 — A Musician's Technique

Preparation: I am not finished with this subject yet. I vividly recall the big, circular music practice rooms at the Indiana University Jacobs School of Music. From early morning at 6:00 a.m. until 11:00 p.m., music students and faculty are constantly practicing. During this time a variety of sounds intertwine—piano, violin, flute, voice, cello, trumpet, etc. We generated quite a sound during these practice sessions. I do not mean that everybody is working out for seventeen hours a day. I am talking about dedication and hard work to perfect the delivery.

I am applying the 120/80 principle here; there is no such phrase as "over-practiced" among musicians. If somebody thinks that they over-practiced, that means they did not practice in a proper way.

You can make your own judgment how much you need to practice your delivery. But I hope the following musician's technique will be useful for your preparation.

Section 1: Vary Your Tempo

The anxiety level on stage decreases dramatically by increasing hours of practice time. It is all relative.

One way to practice presentation is to vary the *tempo* (speed). Musicians are experts on this subject; we practice music in a slower than normal tempo for the following reasons:

- To confirm fingerings (for instrument players)
- To confirm notes and chords
- To confirm breathing
- To master technical difficulties
- To check or feel momentum right before the beginning of the phrase
- To check or feel momentum right after the end of the phrase
- To check our partner's (if any) phrasings
- To feel the climax
- To release tension from nervousness by breathing slower than usual

Similarly, musicians practice music faster than the designated tempo for the following reasons:

- To grasp the big picture of the music as a whole
- To analyze and feel the structure of each phrase

and relationships between various phrases

- To challenge ourselves at technically difficult sections
- To feel the pulse of the music in smaller increments (e.g., feel four beats as one whole entity)

Speech presenters can adopt these musical techniques for similar reasons. We can practice speech scripts slower than conversational speed to confirm the following:

- To confirm words, phrases, and sentences
- To confirm breathing
- To master technical difficulties (e.g., tongue twisters, words that are difficult to pronounce)
- To check or feel momentum (pause) right before the beginning of the phrase or paragraph
- To check or feel momentum (pause) right after the end of the phrase or paragraph
- To check our partner's (if any) phrasings
- To feel the climax
- To release tension from nervousness

By now, I hope you see the strong similarities between music performance and public speaking. Similarly, speakers can practice a script faster than our conversational speed for these reasons:

- To grasp the big picture of the presentation as a whole
- To analyze and feel the structure of each phrase

and the relationships between various phrases

- To challenge technical difficulties (e.g., tongue-twisters, words that are difficult to pronounce)
- To feel the pulse of the speech in smaller increments (e.g., feel four modules as one whole entity)

Music performances and spoken presentations are surprisingly similar. For practice, it is ideal if you can shorten a seven- to ten-minute presentation to less than two minutes by speaking faster. Also, a seven- to ten-minute presentation can be extended to a twenty -minute practice session by speaking slowly. These are good mental and physical exercises to stimulate the brain.

Let's Play Speech!

Section 2: What Is Your Color?

What is the color in your presentation? Black? Red? Green? Musicians imagine color in the music. For instance, there is a famous opening theme of Brahms' *Horn Trio in E-flat Major* (1865), played by a French Horn solo. Whenever I hear that melody, I picture a light mist. I can also see dark green forest in the mist.

Color adds depth to your presentation. What is the color of your scene in the presentation? When you describe your characters or places in the scene, you can also mentally picture specific colors while you say them. Then the audience can also paint the color in their minds. Color is a wonderful element to add in any of your presentations.

Close your eyes and prepare your words. If you still cannot visualize a color, go back and name the colors in your presentation such as "gray concrete wall" or "dark brown eyes." Whichever color is suitable for your feeling, description of your location, and time of day, will help the audience to understand more clearly what you want to say.

Do you feel the color? Don't just say your color. Picture the color in your head. Feel that color while you say it. The relationship between color and emotion is closely tied together. Here are some of the examples of emotion:

- Red: excitement, dynamic, passionate, strong

- Orange: distressing and upsetting
- Purple: dignified and stately
- Yellow: cheerful
- Blue: comfort and security blanket
- Black: sad or angry

Color also describes temperature and warmth. What is your color? Let the audience feel your color and emotion with you.

Section 3: Practice With Scripts

Some musicians memorize the music, some don't. In the orchestra, performers usually do not memorize every symphony. That is normal. In a music ensemble, such as a trio, most musicians don't memorize either.

In a trio or any other ensemble, the pianist usually has a page-turner. In fact, we often joke about a "full-time professional page-turner" who turns the page for renowned artists at Carnegie Hall and other major concert halls. Actually, being a piano page-turner for a famous artist is quite a privilege, because this person is sure to be treated well during the concert.

It is not an easy task to turn music for somebody else. Page-turning requires as much concentration as the pianist. If a turner gets lost in the middle of the music, it is then impossible to turn the page at the appropriate time. Amazingly, all of this activity happens in a split second. A turner cannot turn the page too far ahead of time, but neither can he or she turn the page when the last note of the page has been played. The art of turning must be "just right," and the measure of this "just right" differs among pianists.

By comparison, in a public speech, nobody has a page-turner (wishful thinking here, isn't it?). Obviously, we presenters have to flip our own script pages. Therefore, we need to practice how to be a page-turner.

The advantage here is that the presenter has much more control in turning his or her own pages on the stage than a pianist, and does not need to worry about the page-turner being sick or unable to follow a script.

A music stand (equivalent to "lectern" for a presentation) is usually a black metal rectangle (20.5″ wide, 12.5″ tall) with an adjustable post. Although a piano music stand is physically part of the piano, it is also a standard size; the width and height is pretty much universal no matter which country we go to.

Practicing turning our own script seems to be an easy task. However, it is not that easy. We need to make a conscious effort to flip it at the right moment at the right place. There are a lot of unknowns here:

- Does the facility even have a lectern? (That is the most critical question.)
- What kind of lectern does the event have?
- What is the height of the lectern?
- What is the width of the lectern?
- What is the shape of the lectern?
- What is the lectern made out of? Wood? Glass? Metal?
- Where is the lectern located? Center? Right? Left? Way in the back?
- Can we move the lectern ourselves to a desirable location?
- Who is going to place our script on the lectern?

For all of these questions, we need to be as mentally flexible as possible when we prepare for the presentation. Ask the meeting planner or facility manager ahead of time what kind of lectern they have. If that is not possible, you have to use your own imagination and be as adaptable as possible. If we want, we can use a music stand when we practice at home, and adjust the stand to various heights.

Being a concert performer, I learned that by memorizing sections where pages will be turned—the last line of the page as well as the first line of the following page—my performance will be more successful. This way, even when a page-turner happened to make a mistake, I could still perform my music smoothly.

In terms of public speaking, we have even more flexibility. We can create our script so that difficult sections of the presentation (e.g., referencing third party's quotes, etc.) can be crafted literally in the middle of the page. So when we present that section, we do not have to worry about an interruption in the middle of a large segment. I learned this through my experience as a musician.

Musicians write many comments on their music score—where to breathe, finger numbers, and even color-codes as a reminder when to begin a new phrase. Speech presenters can adopt this technique as well. In the movie *The King's Speech* (2010), I observed King George VI craft extensive notes, arrow signs, pauses, and checkmarks on his script for his famous 1939 radio broadcast "Britain's declaration of War on Germany". Speech is an art. Why not adopt these musician's technique for your next presentation?

How large is the font of your script? If it is too small, you may end up squinting your eyes, which does not make a good impression on the audience, unless that is comically intentional. Printing the script in a large font, usually in the range of 14–20 for letter-size paper, is more desirable.

Crafting a speech while thinking about how to

effectively present this script on stage is an art. By adopting some of the musician's techniques, you will be able to achieve even greater success in your next presentation.

Section 4: Memorization

Memorization. Some presenters hate it, some presenters love it. In the music world, among pianists, memorization is an absolute requirement. Sometimes I wonder, "Why? That is not fair! Why does only a pianist have to memorize and not other instrument players?" However, because of this challenge that I've been experiencing for many years, I can now talk about the value of memorization.

The great benefit of memorization is that we can completely be in that moment and retain full control of ourselves on stage. Musicians do not memorize note by note; we memorize an interpretation. In other words, we work on these following elements simultaneously on every measure of the music:

- Notes
- Speed
- Dynamics and volume
- Sound quality
- Sound balance between notes and chords
- Rhythm
- Phrase and breathing
- Fingerings
- Expression
- Sound balance between left and right hands

- Hand position and posture

By the time we completely understand and master these elements, we realize that we have naturally memorized the music. "Memorize" means "fully understood an interpretation of music," not forcing ourselves to remember the music, note by note.

An important point here: in speaking, by the time we memorize our script, we should have memorized our delivery.

If we say "memorize the script," that means we take each word, remember the order of every word, on every page. "Memorizing the delivery" means we visualize each module of the presentation, prepare each prop, know where we need to stand, where we need to move to on the stage, where to take a pause, and so on. Therefore, we need to memorize both the script and the delivery of the presentation simultaneously.

In order to give our presentation comfortably, we need to run through it (from beginning to end) numerous times. But how do we do that? Some musicians (including myself) rely on a photographic memory. A photographic memory is the ability to vividly recall images with clarity, bordering on actual visual perception.

For example, please take a look at someone close to you: friends, siblings, or parents. Observe this particular person's face carefully for a minute. Now walk away from this same person and close your eyes. Can you picture an image of this person and be able to describe his or her face?

- Color of eyes, hair, skin
- Shape of face

- Hairstyle
- Facial expression—how the mouth moves, how the eyes move

If you can describe them vividly by closing your eyes, congratulations. Your photographic memory is superb. Here is another example: can you read aloud a portion of your presentation script once? Now walk away from this script and close your eyes. Can you picture the following:

- Size of the font.
- What each sentence "looks" like? I'm talking about a visual picture here.
- What each one of the letters or numbers looks like? How do they visually associate with each other?
- Can you visually see the space between each paragraph of your script?

I am not talking about the content of the speech—rather, the actual "look" of the alphanumeric characters within your script. If you can visualize your script, congratulations.

But how about "memorizing the delivery?" Visualize the delivery of your script while following the checklist below when closing your eyes:

- How do you stand on the stage?
- How do you deliver the first word of the script?
- How often and how long do you take a pause?
- How do you pick up and use your props?

These are two different memorization exercises: viewing word by word and sentence by sentence *and* using imagination to describe the delivery of the presentation. When I do these exercises, I visually see a space between each paragraph of a script. When I see that space, I pause. The more you can memorize visually, the more you can easily deliver your speech on stage.

Let's Play Speech!

Section 5: Surprise Quiz Guerrilla Approach

When preparing for a concert, I sometimes approach my piano without any warm-up or preparation, randomly pick a section of music, and start playing to determine if I am capable of delivering it on a professional level.

I call this a "Surprise Quiz." By forcing myself to do this exercise, I am training my mind to adapt to any circumstance. This exercise is similar to improving our reflexes. Video game players can probably relate to this. They have developed their reflexes to give a quick response to any circumstance.

For a speech, I take a similar approach. I pick out a random section of my presentation, present as if I was picking it up from where I "left off," and evaluate if I am physically and mentally capable of delivering it.

I love training my brain in this Guerrilla Approach, so that I can pick up my presentation from anywhere and retain my enthusiasm. I have to admit: I do not yet have a 100 percent success rate for this mental exercise on the piano. Whenever I randomly pick a piano section with a lot of chords running up and down in both hands simultaneously, I am often thinking "Oh my goodness! Oh my goodness! How can I play this? I need twenty fingers to get there." Just imagine driving a car. When we start a car, it usually accelerates gradually, from 0 mph, to 5 mph, and eventually 25 mph in a matter of a minute or so.

What I am proposing as the Guerrilla Approach is as if

my car hits the road at 50 mph within the first one to two seconds. Musicians do this mental exercise on a regular basis using their own instruments. I've been around enough musicians so that I'm no longer surprised when opera singers suddenly start singing a segment of their song in the middle of the hallway (or any public place).

The Guerilla Approach works! However, it requires some trial and error. If I happen to fail in the middle of this exercise, I don't stop it. Rather, I improvise when I'm delivering a speech, and I skip a note when I am playing piano. The goal here is to produce something meaningful and presentable on the fly.

Section 6: Do You Really Mean It?

Whenever I practice music, I ask myself between each phrase:

- "Do I really mean it?"
- "Am I presenting an accurate interpretation for the audience?"
- "Am I sharing the right emotions or just pushing the keyboard meaninglessly without emotion?"
- "Did I demonstrate the scene, using the right color as it is described in the music score?"

When I am on stage, I am responsible for every sound I create. If the audience is not convinced by my delivery, I have not succeeded.

I talked about feeling in the First Movement. I am going a step further now. "Do I really mean it? Do I mean how I feel?"

Music comes from the heart. Music is essentially a form of expression. For example, there is a passage in Schumann's piano music *Fantasie in C*. In this music, Schumann expresses his frustration of being separated from his girlfriend, Clara. He is frustrated. He is sad and angry, and that feeling is demonstrated with the burst of left-hand arpeggios, along with a longing phrase of the right hand. When I play this music, I have to ask myself, "Does my music sound as if Schumann is expressing his frustration and sadness?" If not, I fail to "mean it," and I will most likely disappoint the audience with my poor interpretation. I need to practice until I can feel his agony. Also, when I catch myself not "meaning it" during my practice, I usually think "why don't I mean it?"

In order to resolve a situation, we can answer the question, "Why don't I mean it?" with more specific questions, such as:

- Why was I not concentrating on this note?
- Why did my phrase suddenly die at this section?
- Why am I trying to emphasize the left hand when the right hand must dominate this section?

My answers to the "Why don't I mean it?" question might include the following:

- My cat distracted me while I was playing this note.
- My hand tripped when I was trying to turn a page.
- I am having difficulty with left-hand sequences. I need to work on technical problems separately.

To diagnose a problem, a "Why" question is more effective than a "What" question. A "What" question is relatively easy to answer (i.e., missed a particular note, pause too short, pause too long, wrong expression, etc.). With a "What" question, we can state a fact and spot a certain flaw of the presentation. I find the "Why" question extremely difficult to answer sometimes, because it requires us to go deeper in our thinking process. When I figure out the "Why" question, I usually jump up and down, because these answers are the key to resolving my real problem.

Then, the next question will come: "How can I mean it?" This "How" can be answered by the following actions:

- I can place my cat in a separate room while I am practicing.
- I can synchronize my hands and turn the page at the end of the phrase. Eventually, I can memorize this section to minimize the problem.
- I can work on left-hand sequences separately to the point that sequences feel comfortable enough to create music together with the right hand.

This musician's principle is easy to apply to public speaking. For example, if you are presenting a talk about a joyful moment of reuniting with your mother, do you really mean it? Do you feel the joy? Can you be in that moment? Can you make the audience rejoice with you in your happy moment? Where is your emotion coming from?

Now, in your presentation, do you really mean what you say? If you say something which does not match with your body gestures or facial expression, the audience will notice that as fake. There is no credibility. How do you practice that?

This process requires imagination. We want to be in our own Time Machine. We want to be in that moment. We want to be as sincere as possible in describing that particular moment which happened in our own life.

Picture yourself facing your mother, for example. What was your mother's expression? What did you say? Picture everything that happened, even details which may not be in your script. If your mother is not present while you are actually practicing, how can you recreate that special joy?

Do you mean it? If yes, congratulations. If not, "Why don't you mean it?" Make sure to find reasons why a particular delivery is not successful. And most importantly, "How can I mean it?" Finding solutions to "Why" questions dramatically helps to conquer mental weaknesses. "Why" and "How": these are important questions to think about as we prepare for the presentation.

Fourth Movement

Basic Logistics — A Musician's Backstage

One day, I performed on the stage as part of a trio: piano, violin, and cello. For the concert, I wore a beautiful, stylish, professional-looking black top with sparkling-silver buttons and a matching skirt. I looked great. The only problem…five minutes before our presentation, I realized that my skirt was very short. That day, I was more nervous about my skirt than my performance. This was an embarrassing situation. I could not concentrate on my music throughout the performance and felt miserable on the stage.

What I am going to describe in this Fourth Movement are basic logistics—what to wear, what to bring, etc. I feel very strongly about this topic. These basics will make a big difference in our performance on the stage.

This section is a result of a lot of the trial and error over my years of piano performances. I hope it is helpful.

Section 1: What to Wear — Shoes

In many years of performing, I strongly believe that the kind of shoes we wear is the most critical aspect of our presentation. Actually, the audience is unlikely to focus on our shoes when we are up on the stage. Therefore, our shoes do not have to be one of the most stylish high-end shoes of the year (unless you are walking on the red carpet at the Academy Awards).

The most important question here is, how comfortable are my shoes? Can I walk comfortably? Can I even run comfortably? If we can run with the shoes we wear, then in any situation we can move around energetically. Therefore, I take a lot of my time choosing the right shoes for my presentation.

Particularly for women, if we wear high heels, we cannot wear wobbly-heeled shoes. It looks unstable and fragile on the stage. An audience will feel uneasy about any instability of foot movement throughout our presentation. I once saw a presentation given by a gorgeous-looking woman with stylish high heels. Every time she walked on stage, she just looked wobbly, period. I was so focused on her high heels that I do not remember what she presented that day. Her wobbly-heeled shoes did not provide a solid foundation for her feet, or give her a solid posture. If high heels cannot sustain the weight of the whole body, we do not want to wear those particular shoes. We need to be grounded; that is the key. Don't go for the fanciest shoes of the year, unless those shoes make you feel grounded.

If you still prefer wearing the latest high-heel shoes, I highly recommend practicing walking and running in the shoes many times even before practicing your presentation. Good luck!

I prefer rubber soles on a wooden stage, because rubber soles eliminate extra sound. If rubber soles are not an option for you, you can try shoes with non-slippery leather soles which do not generate noise on a wooden floor.

I know a pianist who flew from Japan to San Francisco, went to a party, went on a short hike, and finally gave a concert *all in one day with that same pair of shoes*. It was a pair of simple, black suede loafers. I vividly remember what her shoes looked like. She was breathing and living with the same shoes for twenty-four hours (her piano performance was magnificent that night as well).

My favorite is Clarks' black or brown classical heel. I usually invest some money in good shoes which last for many years. However, everybody has their own taste and knows what feels right. Ask your feet which shoes are most comfortable.

I test my shoes on a wooden floor before I purchase them. If the shoes generate too much noise when I walk around, it will distract the audience, so I will not consider them, no matter how comfortable they are.

You may want to spend extra time checking shoelaces to make sure the material is reliable and won't untie easily. Personally, I avoid wearing shoes with shoelaces. I don't want to end up tying shoelaces every ten minutes during my presentation. Obviously, for men, this may not be an option. Invest money in good quality shoelaces which are not too long, so you, or somebody else, won't trip on them while walking.

Investing in a good quality, "quiet," and comfortable pair of shoes is the most critical first step toward our next presentation. If you have a pair, that is great! If you do not, it is about time to think about asking your feet and sole (soul as well).

Section 2: What to Wear — Clothes

Just like our shoes, our outfit does not have to follow the latest fashion from the Paris Collection. Rather, I prefer clothes which do not choke the neck. I also avoid clothes which restrict movements of shoulders, arms, wrists, ankles, knees, legs, back, waist, and fingers. This is critical to any musical performance, especially for a pianist who is sitting on the chair throughout.

You might think it is not a big deal what you wear on the stage. Oh no, that is not true! We have to plan way ahead of time what we wear…plan it and practice the performance with these clothes. We have to be good friends with our clothes.

I like a basic black suit with pants. Some women prefer a suit with a skirt. Color and materials are up to the individual. Men usually wear a suit with matching tie (or no tie for a casual occasion). Again, style and color depends upon each person's taste.

If you wait until the day of the presentation to choose your outfit, you will be met with unexpected surprises. I once presented a speech in front of a large crowd in a public library. I chose one of my favorite suit jackets. It was light-grey wool, and looked sharp on me. When I started rehearsing with this jacket, I felt uncomfortable reaching my arms in front of me. It was a little snug, which made me uncomfortable. Although I love this jacket very much, I decided not to wear it for my presentation.

Please do not choose clothes just because they look gorgeous and follow the latest trends. Ask your body how comfortable your outfit is when you are:

- Standing straight
- Walking around
- Running
- Jumping
- Bending over
- Reaching arms to the side and in front
- Reaching arms over the head
- Picking up props
- Taking a deep breath
- Speaking
- Laughing
- Shouting

In order to answer these questions, you may need to spend time rehearsing with your outfit (along with the shoes described in the previous section). If anything you wear bothers you or causes distraction, please consider plan B. Here are some examples:

- Scarf is falling off of my shoulder every five minutes
- Jacket makes noise every time I raise my arms
- Shirt collar chokes me
- Belt is too tight

Please do not underestimate the effect of your wardrobe on stage. Make a good decision and shine on stage!

Section 3: Water

Water is essential for any presentation. Simple room-temperature water is the key. No ice water, no fancy, flavored water. Ice water will make your vocal cords tense. Flavored water is nice, but may not be practical and economical (unless you already have one available). Keep a bottle of room-temperature water handy and bring it wherever you give your presentation.

I once arrived at a conference room that was extremely cozy and comfortable. That made me relaxed, and I completely forgot about my water bottle. Yes, I walked on the stage without my water.

My presentation went miserably. My mouth was completely dry, and I could not project my voice. I choked, and I was stuck in the middle of the sentence. And I did not have my water! No! Help!

You may think it is not a big deal. No, it is a big deal. If you cannot physically project your voice for the first five to ten minutes, the audience may walk out the door during your performance.

Water is definitely a must. If you cannot physically access water, please make sure your assistant or hosts can provide water prior to your presentation.

Section 4: What to Bring — Props

Previously, I discussed how to handle props. Now let's put it into action. Prepare a list of props for your presentation; make sure they are all well-maintained and ready to go.

This reminder may be very simple; however, if you do *not* have a checklist and forget any of your props (e.g., the flash drive for your PowerPoint presentation), you may be in trouble on the stage.

There is no going back. Please do not forget to make a checklist. You'll be surprised how much "stuff" you need to take to your next presentation.

A side note: there is a famous story about my teacher, Judy Carter. Judy started out as a successful magician; yes, she is an absolutely amazing presenter. On one occasion, her luggage full of props did not show up at the gate of the airport.

What would you do if that happened to you? If I were her, I might panic and cancel the event! In her case, the tragedy turned to her advantage. She presented joke after joke, and her audience did not want her to leave! Not only did she survive, she thrived to become a well-known Comedy Queen.

No matter how much you have prepared, mishaps—such as losing an entire suitcase—may occasionally happen; in that case, well, we all want to be as flexible as Judy and become successful in any circumstances.

Fifth Movement

How to Own the Stage — A Musician's Performance

By now, you probably have noticed—my intent in this book is focused on the delivery of the presentation and mindset of the delivery. Yes, mindset: 90 percent of delivery is mindset. The other 10 percent is preparation.

Of course, that is not all we need to become a fabulous presenter. Also, the more we give presentations, the more we improve our presentation skills. Just having the mindset will not work. In a previous section, I stressed the 120/80 principle.

I am shy by nature. When I was in kindergarten, a teacher told my mother that I was hopeless at not being able to speak in front of people. The teacher also recommended to my parents that I need to do some activities, either piano or ballet. I personally do not remember these remarks. But one day, I saw a piano in our living room, so I bet that I said "piano" as my choice of hobby.

However, my shyness does not stop me from motivating others and influencing people. In some way, both music and public speaking made me break out of my little shell. Some say that I blossom on stage, and some say I am funny on stage.

How do I do that? As I mentioned earlier, everything is mindset. I will share the mindset that has worked for me. I hope this will work for you, too.

Section 1: Acoustics

Have you ever thought about the acoustics of the place you give your presentation? Acoustics is defined by Merriam-Webster as the science that deals with the production, control, transmission, reception, and effects of sound.

Acoustics are the most critical challenge for every musician. What determines either good or fair acoustics depends on:

- Size of the hall or room
- Number of chairs and tables in the hall
- Height of the ceiling
- Size of the stage
- Size of the audience
- …Even the temperature of the room

In every place I perform, I arrive early and clap my hands on the stage. I wish I could snap my fingers (I can't); that would be even better and I would look so cool! When I clap, I ask myself these questions:

- Does the sound bounce back to me?
- How fast does my sound come back to me?
- How loud is my sound when it comes back to me?
- Where does my sound come back from?

- Can anybody else hear my clap?

In a place with "dead" and "dry" acoustics, where there is no sound bouncing back to me, I take it as a challenge. If this is my speech, my voice may get absorbed by the room. Furthermore, I ask myself these questions after I clap:

- Is the stage carpeted?
- Is the stage a wooden floor?
- Is the stage a laminate floor or something special?
- Is the stage raised or an equal height to the audience?
- Is the audience section carpeted?
- Is the audience section a wooden floor?
- How big is the room?
- How high is the ceiling?
- How bright or dark is the room?
- Does any wall have windows?
- Does any wall have draperies?

If both the stage and audience sections are a wooden floor, most likely there will be more ring to my clap, since floor reflects more sound. If we have more acoustics, we have more echoes. Sound rings back, so we may have to speak slower to make sure everybody in the room can hear our every word and sentence clearly.

In addition to this, presenters have to be aware of microphones. A combination of the acoustics plus a microphone adds complexity to our delivery. If there is too much echo in the room, the microphone may be a challenging device to use. Contacting the audio crew ahead of time will relieve tension and stress on your side.

Back to the acoustics. When your ears are used to sound around you, it is an advantage when giving an effective presentation. Prior to the actual presentation, you can also pay attention to:

- How much sound does your audience generate? With echo? No echo? Ringing? Dry?
- How loud are the voices of the audience?
- What kind of noise do you hear besides the audience? What do you do about the noise if it continues during your presentation?

Listen to your voice, listen to surrounding voices, and be sensitive to any sound you hear around you.

Section 2: Mindset — Please Give Me an *A*

When we musicians play in an ensemble, we walk together onto the stage and start with a mutual agreement: Please give me the note *A*.

Then the pianist or violinist will play the middle *A* on the keyboard. The piano keyboard's tone *A* becomes the focal point prior to the presentation. Each performer needs to make sure to listen to this *A* and adjust their own instruments to the same pitch as the Hertz of the piano.

I am telling you this because this moment when musicians cue each other to receive the note *A* becomes a valuable time of relaxation as well as a time of mental preparation. The final mental check occurs during these five seconds of activity.

When you are on stage, within the first five seconds, what do you do to mentally prepare yourself? For a presenter, I believe the best time for this relaxation is when you are being introduced by the host, MC, or whoever runs your event. If you want to have a longer period of relaxation, you can intentionally craft your own longer introduction!

On stage, the moment you shake the host's hands starts this period of "relaxation." Those five seconds are your *A* moment. What is in your mind in those five seconds?

- "I am excited to be on this platform with my dear audience."
- "I am terrified."
- "I forgot to eat my dinner. I'm hungry."
- "I left my keys in my car…"

Of course, everything except the first one listed above is not desirable.

How do you give your A? This important initial five seconds will make or break the rest of your presentation. By calmly standing in front of the audience and having your own peaceful A moment, you will definitely own the stage. Cheers and congratulations.

Section 3: How to Own the Stage

Owning the stage means you are fully in control of yourself while on stage. But what does it mean? Actually, it is how you feel the stage.

During your performance, how quickly can you feel the following within the first five seconds on center stage?

- The size of the stage
- The size of the audience
- The type of target audience
- The acoustics of the room
- The lighting of the stage and the entire room
- The type of the room (as discussed earlier)

Grasping these aspects within the first five seconds you take center stage is critical. No matter how well you prepare your presentation, the atmosphere on stage with a live audience is quite different from any rehearsal session. It is a performer's responsibility to absorb and feel the stage as quickly as possible.

The list above is my checklist for music performances. After I am on the stage and receiving the welcoming applause, I usually do not start my music until I quickly check the list and confirm that I am fully aware of all of these conditions.

The audience will be paying attention to your every move and listening to your every sound (or word). The quicker you can absorb these aspects, the sooner you will own the stage.

This checklist is the first phase. The next phase when you are on stage is to share information with your audience. How do we do that? Based on the checklist, our mind should be consciously adjusting and re-adjusting our presentation to accommodate this particular audience.

One day, I had to perform piano in a hall where the size of the audience was over five hundred people— much larger than expected. That particular day, I had to make a quick judgment to play the music "bigger" than usual. Another example was when a concert planner suddenly decided to move the concert to in front of a fancy entryway to a historic castle. The change was made suddenly on the day of the concert. This entryway happened to have a lot of echoes and poor acoustics. Almost too much echo for music! Therefore, I had to make a quick decision not to use the piano pedal (i.e., the pedal that sustains the piano sound and was not desirable in this circumstance).

Remember, this mental checklist exercise needs to happen within the first five seconds you are on stage. How do you feel after reviewing the checklist? If you feel good, that is great. If you do not feel good, there can be many reasons:

- Could not sleep well the night before
- Could not eat well prior to the event
- Physical problems (e.g., stomach ache)
- Lighting too bright or too dim
- Audience not paying attention
- …and so on

Sometimes nervousness and stage fright appear unexpectedly because of a very small incident such as I described above. If these conditions do not get resolved quickly and promptly, your nervousness may get worse and worse throughout your presentation. To prevent this from happening, consider the following options:

- Take a deep breath
- Slowly rotate and relax your shoulders
- Ask somebody to bring water for you
- Picture a big smiley face in front of you, then smile to the audience
- Imagine this is your own living room
- Believe that the audience is there to support you
- Ask for help to make adjustments to technical problems (e.g., light casting shadow on your script)
- Recite your take-away message in your head three times
- Bow to your audience

...Then start your first line with power! Owning the stage requires mental exercises, concentration, and quick adjustments.

Let's Play Speech!

Section 4: Mental Strength

One day, I was practicing a difficult melody on the piano, leaping from the low note *A* to the high note *C* with my right hand. Then I missed hitting the last high note *C*. This happened the day before my concert performance. What did I do? Before the concert, I was thinking about this last high note *C*. "I missed high *C*, I missed high *C*…"

Guess what happened at the live performance? Yes, I missed high *C*. I needed to have 100 percent conviction, with absolutely *no* doubt in my mind during the performance. If I think that I will mess up at note *C*, I will mess it up. It is all psychological.

Have you seen practice runs of figure skaters at the World Championships or Olympics? I have seen them many times on TV. These athletes usually work on their challenging spins and jumps during the practice session. I have noticed that when they do not do the spin and jumps well on the practice day before the competition, their chance of failing at the actual competition is relatively high.

This does not mean that they are mediocre skaters. I am confident that all of these wonderful skaters possess incredible talent and technique. However, what separates the first-place winner from the second-place winner is their superior mental strength. The importance of the psychological factor during a live performance is enormous. The fact is, the technique, skill and talent of all first-, second-, and third-place winners in athletics can be almost identical or a split-millisecond difference. However, what sets them apart is mental strength and flexibility. If a skater starts out thinking "I'll mess up," sure enough, they'll mess up. Remember the Stripper's Walk? I have observed the same principle in these world-class figure skaters as well. It is all mental.

My peers and fellow musicians study figure skaters presentation techniques in great detail. We check the mental strength of each athlete—not only his or her artistic elegance and techniques. We can immediately identify the mental strength of the world-class skater, not only the technical ability or artistic talent. For these reasons, we need to train our mental capacities to become world-class presenters.

One day, after practicing a piece of piano music, I kept thinking "This section is too difficult, I can't make it." While thinking that way, my practice was unpleasant. My negative attitude eventually showed on the stage, and my performance of that particular piece of music was unsuccessful.

Musicians and performing artists, as well as athletes, are mentally trained to think as "You are number 1." No, I am not joking here. That is part of the training, thinking that you are the best of the world. How is your mental strength? It is a very important factor in performance.

Section 5: Handle Nervousness

We musicians are trained to handle nervousness on stage. Obviously, the more often we perform on stage, the more comfortable we become. It is like riding a bicycle. The more we pedal, the further we can go. One way to handle nervousness is to completely absorb the silent moment immediately before we perform. We need to enjoy this moment and own this silence. Silently repeat:

"This stage is mine."
"This moment is mine."

Then take a deep breath. The more oxygen we have, the more our body and mind will relax.

Be in that moment.

Before I play the very first note of music on stage, I quickly review what my entire piece of music will sound like, as if I am watching a sneak preview of the movie. When this happens, I can look forward to sharing my music with my audience.

Be in that moment.

Then nervousness will be reduced dramatically on stage.

It is normal to get nervous and frightened on stage for any of the following reasons:

- Lack of practice and preparation
- Unfamiliar audience

- Unfriendly audience
- Audience with no reaction to your presentation
- Small audience
- Unexpectedly large audience
- Unexpected mishaps (e.g., PowerPoint malfunction)
- Being late for the presentation
- Shy personality

Distractions are one of the bigger reasons why people get nervous on stage such as:

- Somebody dropped an object on floor and made a noise
- Light suddenly switched on or off
- Child crying
- Phone ringing

If we let these things distract us from our presentations, we will fail. Why? Because these distractions will derail our thought process, and eventually the audience will sense that our mind is not there.

The more we lose our concentration, the more nervous we become. The more nervous we become, the more we start to doubt ourselves.

When distractions occur, we may want to ignore them. Let them pass without acknowledging them to the audience. Then, by the end of the presentation, the audience will have forgotten the incident.

Be in that moment.

In a Zen temple, monks are encouraged to think about nothing. Have you tried thinking about nothing? I have done it, and failed miserably. I always find myself thinking about daily concerns when I need to sit and meditate during my Yoga practice. It is very difficult to fully commit myself to think about nothing. In fact, thinking about nothing is the one of the most difficult tasks to do in our lives. We are always occupied with thoughts and doubts in our mind.

Be in that moment.

It is also a myth that a shy people cannot present on a stage. Shy people are simply not accustomed to speaking in front of the public. As long as they have a strong message to share *and* have a strong *desire* to share, they can overcome shyness. It is all a matter of choice. Of course, shy people may require double the amount of effort of naturally extroverted people. However, if shy people have conviction and 120 percent concentration on stage, I am certain that they will be well received.

Please refer to the previous 120/80 Principle of my Second Movement, Section 1 in this regard.

Be in that moment.

We don't have to possess a tremendous focus like a Zen monk to be a great presenter; however, we do need 120 percent concentration and to put our body and soul 120 percent into the presentation. That is the essential key to success.

Be in that moment.

Section 6: Nervousness—Ignore Your Heartbeat

Do you feel your heartbeat on stage during your presentation? How fast is it? How slow is it? Believe it or not, our heartbeat can dominate our presentation, no matter if we are presenting music or speech. Our heartbeat can set a rhythm for the entire presentation. If our heartbeat speeds up, we may accidentally deliver our presentation much faster than we intend to. As a result, we may confuse our audience.

A fast heartbeat is a major symptom of the fear of presenting in public. Why does this happen? Because people feel at risk and physically overreact to the sudden change in the environment (e.g., a change from a living room to an auditorium with a seating capacity of 1,000).

In order to combat this, we need to take action. When you start feeling that your heart is beating too fast, you need to send a signal to your body to slow down your presentation. When our heartbeat speeds up, we need to become aware of it. We need to resist the feeling it brings and learn to ignore our heartbeat.

Musicians like to say: "When you feel you are slowing down, play your music even slower." Ignoring our racing heart requires tremendous mental strength and experience, because this symptom is psychological.

The heartbeat syndrome happens on stage with a live audience. You may think you are delivering at a slow pace; however, sometimes it may actually be faster than you know.

One way to experiment with this at home is to create anxiety before you practice your presentation. What I mean is this—picture a moment or incident in the past which made your heartbeat pound such as:

- Being late for an important meeting or job interview
- Witnessing a car accident
- Being involved in car accident
- Death of a loved one
- And so on…

In order to combat a racing heartbeat on a big stage, you need to simulate a state of mind at home that triggers nervousness. This is very important, because nervousness followed by fast heartbeat usually only happens during live performances. Can you practice your presentation in this state of mind? With this state of mind, can you learn to ignore your heartbeat?

It is also helpful to record or video tape yourself each time you present. When you examine your tape after your presentation, see if you can remember how your heartbeat felt on stage. It is interesting to study how fast or slow you spoke relative to your heartbeat that particular day.

The good news is that the more opportunities you have to present, your heartbeat will slow down. Just remember, while on the stage, feel the resistance.

Ignore your heartbeat.

Section 7: Gesture

Have you seen a conductor swinging his or her arms to start a performance? For a big sound, a conductor swings his arms with a big gesture. For a small sound, a small arm gesture.

Gesture is fundamental to music making. Arm gestures are not just for conductors. Pianists, cellists, violinists, and other musicians all prepare their gestures before playing notes or phrases.

I am petite—5'2". In fact, my bicycle is the biggest kid's size! And yet, people often comment that I have a good stage presence, and I look bigger on stage. Why? In order to look bigger on stage, I use my entire body. Now, how do I use the entire body? By making big gestures. By moving my arms to their full capacity. When I extend both of my arms side by side, that is approximately the length of my height, 5'2". I take full advantage of this extension of my arms during my presentation.

How should we use gestures effectively to convey our message successfully?

When I play piano music, my feet are firmly set on the ground, my back is straight, my arms are extended. My shoulders are relaxed.

Now I prepare my gestures.

I prepare a big sound with big swings of my arms. That's how I generate the sound of heavy chords on the piano. Large, full sound comes from the keyboard because of big gestures.

If I relied solely on my finger power to play the piano, my music would sound like a mosquito humming. That is not very effective.

When speaking, we can use gestures in a similar fashion. Back straight. Feet firmly on the floor. Chest forward. Chin high. **Relax those shoulders.** What is your facial expression five seconds before you walk onto the stage? Touch and feel your face to make sure it is relaxed.

Now, extend your arms to the entire audience. The more relaxed your shoulders and arms are, the more you can give your presentation with ease. Big arm gestures will add power to your presentation for a large audience.

When we have an intimate conversation with another person, we want to minimize our gestures. We do not have to move our arms around when we talk privately, do we? Well, maybe we do if we are Italian! Bravo!

Your gesture will become a beautiful piece of art when you are relaxed. When that happens, I am sure that your audience will be mesmerized and captivated by your presentation.

Let's Play Speech!

Section 8: Dialogue

I learned about dialogue through performing music. Among musicians on the stage, there are many kinds of dialogue:

- Dialogue performed by a solo musician
- Dialogue performed by multiple musicians (e.g., violinist and pianist; pianist and orchestra)
- Dialogue performed by a performer, then the audience

Dialogue by a solo performer? Yes, this is possible on the piano. For example, let's go back to Schumann's piano music *Fantasie in C*. There is a section of soprano (high) melody followed by a series of bass (low) melodies. The soprano is the voice of Clara, longing to see Schumann, and the bass is the voice of Schumann, longing to see Clara. These conversations are played by the right hand (Clara) and the left hand (Schumann). In the finale, both hands play together as a duet.

A dialogue between two musicians gets a bit tricky. This requires that the musician not only practice their own part, but also become aware of what their partner might do unexpectedly during the live performance.

Again, I want to consider "What if..."

- My partner plays one phrase too loudly?

- My partner starts to play faster than expected?
- My partner takes a longer pause than I expected?

A musician needs to quickly detect these factors on stage and respond accordingly:

Then...

- I will follow my partner to play louder
- I will play slower than my partner and lead our performance in order not to lose control
- I will listen carefully and wait

When speaking, there are similar concepts about dialogue:

- Dialogue spoken by a single presenter (you)
- Dialogue between a presenter (you) and another presenter on the stage
- Dialogue between a presenter (you) and the audience

Here are some possibilities to consider about the musician's approach.

For a dialogue spoken by a single presenter, make a distinction in your voice between different characters by doing the following:

- Review the personality of each character
- Review the vocal range of each character
- Study what each character is thinking during the dialogue

- Review each character's feelings before and after the dialogue
- Confirm the background of each character (e.g., age, education, etc.)

Here is a "What if..." list to consider for dialogue between more than one person:

- I will follow my partner to speak louder
- I will speak slower than my partner to differentiate a character
- I will listen carefully and wait
- If my partner makes a joke, joke back as a response

Once you have mastered these elements in your presentation, dialogue will become more interesting to you and entertaining for your audience.

Section 9: Improvisation

Have you seen jazz musicians' music scores? There are practically no notes on the score for several pages. They fill in the blanks themselves as they perform.

Jazz musicians are the kings of improvisation. They know how to "make things up" in a proper way, so their presentations are convincing. I have one of the music scores for Dave Brubeck Quartet's *Charlie Brown*. I often wonder how these geniuses can be so flexible every time they perform this piece of music. Since the music scores are blank, each of their performances is slightly different every time they perform it.

In music, the best improvisation strategy is that no matter what happens, stay focused, keep the tempo steady, and do not stop until the end of music. This is absolutely critical, especially when multiple musicians play together as an ensemble. Among musicians, we always say, "Don't drop it." If I can keep up with the steady tempo, I can say I am succeeding approximately 90 percent in making music. Even if I miss a note or two, I don't want to waste time thinking and analyzing missed notes. We do not have time to reflect. In other words, keep moving forward, the notes follow the tempo.

How can we apply this musical improvisation technique to spoken presentations? It can be done by intentionally leaving part of your speech script with "blank" pages. Therefore, every time you present this "blank" section, your presentation will be unique.

Then the question arises, is it appropriate to improvise when you present? Absolutely. In some cases, since each presentation is unique, it will always sound fresh. The trick is that you don't just leave your script blank. You still have to have an outline of what you need to talk about as a high level plan in your head (or a written outline) prior to your presentation.

Here are some tips. Try to remember how you walked on the stage, including:

- Sound of your footsteps (sound of your *pulse*)
- Intervals of each step (measure of your *pulse*)
- How fast or slow you walked (tempo of your *pulse*)

Make a mental note of the *pulse* you created during your grand entrance. Feel this *pulse* as the presentation progresses. When your presentation comes to the blank section of the script, immediately outline your agenda for this blank section in the next three seconds. Then take action, such as one of the following:

- Walk to a different part of the stage and keep feeling your *pulse*
- Walk toward the audience in the front and keep feeling your *pulse*
- Walk toward the center aisle (if any) and keep feeling your *pulse*
- Stay where you are, take a deep breath, and keep feeling your *pulse*

The main point here is "don't drop" the pulse throughout the presentation. Keep feeling it.

While this *pulse* is happening, you can improvise your presentation any way you wish, such as the following:

- Show the audience a new prop
- Dance
- Give a pop quiz to the audience
- Tell a joke
- Give handouts
- Ask questions to the audience
- Bring audience members onto the stage
- Show a video or slides
- Play music
- …and much, much more!

By "not dropping" your pulse, you can stay focused and positive. By keeping your pulse, you will not be mentally distracted about missed modules or ideas. This is all psychological. Please "do not drop" your presentation.

Improvisation. This is an advanced skill for any presenter. If you think you are ready for it, test it out and evaluate if this is the right style of presentation for you.

Section 10: How to Respond to Audience Reaction

During a classical music concert, the audience is silently listening to our performance. We cherish this moment. We also feel the power of intensity, the power of concentration, and the power of excitement, all coming from the audience. Yes, we can feel this, even though the audience is quiet.

Take the last chord of Schumann's *Fantasie in C*. This soft, gentle chord symbolizes a unity between Clara and Schumann. When we perform this last chord, we can feel that the audience is at peace. By generating this sound and listening to the resonance of the cadence, performer and audience share the same happiness. There is an invisible power within us, between performer and audience, sharing a beautiful moment together during the performance. We become one with the universe. This sensation is incredible. This is a sacred moment for both musicians and audience.

In spoken presentations, we can also share a beautiful moment together with our audience. Picture yourself giving a speech about being in that moment of peace— being united with your loved one. If you can describe that moment accurately, sincerely, with expressive conversational voice, your audience will be with you, feeling the same happiness. This becomes your sacred moment.

It is almost like throwing and catching a ball between a

presenter and the audience. You also anticipate that the audience will laugh in a certain part of your presentation. We actually love these interruptions from the audience. Unpredictable interruptions make our presentation lively.

When I practice my presentations, both piano *and* speech, sometimes I place ordinary household objects in front of me and present to them. I might use my mug, my stuffed teddy bear, or a group of chairs. Just imagine that the object is a person. Present to them; you have to really present *to* them. Don't present *at* them. Of course, there will not be a response from these objects, but use them to practice so that you anticipate different responses and be ready with an answer. For example:

After I say "A",

- If response (from the audience) is *B*, then do *C*
- If response is *D*, then do *F*
- If there is no response, then do *Z*
- If there is laughter in section *A*, then pause this much and do *Y*
- ...and so on.

Imagine that your household objects are responding with different answers. By practicing anticipated responses in advance, we are preparing to respond with flexibility. By not limiting ourselves to a one-sided presentation, preparing different versions of our response makes it easier to react when we are live on the stage. Enjoy responses. Enjoy beautiful moments together.

Let's Play Speech!

Sixth Movement

Encore — A Musician's Moment

It's said among musicians that the best time to improve a performance is immediately after giving it. In other words, the moment we come off stage, if we have the energy and time to give the same presentation once again, our skill will improve dramatically.

The reason is that we are still in a "performance" state of mind. We know our material by heart, it's fresh in our brain, and it's fresh in the moment. We can feel the audience reaction. Our entire body remembers the exciting journey.

If the time allows, within twenty-four hours, I highly encourage you to give the presentation twice, the first is the live performance, then with no audience or a few people of your choice. I guarantee, the second time around flows much more smoothly. By then, you may well be thinking "Ah! Why didn't I do that an hour ago for five hundred people? I like the second one much better!"

If you ever do this, please make sure to record yourself both times.

Every musician has buddies, a master, teacher, professor, mentor, or coach, who can provide constructive feedback and suggestions. All the great performers and artists have a coach. Find people that you can trust and give a rehearsal for them. Their constructive feedback is extremely valuable. If you don't have one, start looking for a coach right now. I am sure that he or she can assist you in finding your own voice.

This is the musician's approach.

Let's Play Speech!

I wish you the best for your next presentation.

Intermission

About the Author

Using her expertise as a musician, Emiko Hori gives presentations about the relationship between music performance and public speaking.

As a graduate of renowned Indiana University Jacobs School of Music in Bloomington, Indiana, Emiko has performed piano recitals throughout the U.S., Europe, and Canada including master classes in Bergamo, Italy; the Banff Centre for the Arts in Canada; the Schleswig-Holstein Musik Festival in Germany, and others.

Her biggest influences while writing this book have been pianists Marek Jablonski, Shigeo Neriki, and György Sebők, the author of *The Comedy Bible* and *The Message Of You,* Judy Carter, and the 2001 World Champion of Public Speaking, Darren LaCroix.

http://www.LetsPlaySpeech.com

Version History 3.0
December 2013

Postlude

References

What is Acoustics?, Brigham Young University Department of Physics & Astronomy, BYU Acoustics Research Group. 2013.
http://www.physics.byu.edu/research/acoustics/what_is _acoustics.aspx

The Essential 20: Twenty Components of an Excellent Health Care Team, Dukette, Dianne and David Cornish. 2009. RoseDog Books. ISBN 1-4349-9555-0.

Jacobs School of Music, Indiana University, Bloomington, IN 47405. http://music.indiana.edu/

Relationship between color and emotion: a study of college students, Kaya, Naz and Helen H. Epps. 2004. College Student Journal, Vol. 38, No. 3.
http://www.freepatentsonline.com/article/College-Student-Journal/123321897.html

Stand-Up Comic Helps Employees Deal With Stress in the Workplace, Kranhold, Kathryn. 1997. Wall Street Journal. http://judycarter.com/pdf/general/WallStreet.pdf

Schumann: Fantasie, Op. 17., Marston, Nicholas. 1992. Cambridge: Cambridge University Press. ISBN 0-521-39892-4.

Please give me an A, Neriki, Shigeo. 2003. Shunjusha. ISBN 4-393-93476-8.

Marek Jablonski (1939-1999): Light and shadow, La Scena Musicale5(6), Renaud, Lucie. 2000. http://www.scena.org/lsm/sm5-6/Jablonski-en.htm

Girl, 14, Conquers Tanglewood with 3 Violins, Rockwell, John. 1986. New York Times, Late City Final Edition, Section A, Page 1, Column 3. http://www.nytimes.com/1986/07/28/arts/girl-14-conquers-tanglewood-with-3-violins.html